Happy Holidays!
Juneteenth

by Rebecca Sabelko

BELLWETHER MEDIA
MINNEAPOLIS, MN

Blastoff! Beginners are developed by literacy experts and educators to meet the needs of early readers. These engaging informational texts support young children as they begin reading about their world. Through simple language and high frequency words paired with crisp, colorful photos, Blastoff! Beginners launch young readers into the universe of independent reading.

Sight Words in This Book

about	eat	is	the
and	for	it	they
black	from	on	time
called	go	people	to
day	in	red	up

This edition first published in 2023 by Bellwether Media, Inc.

No part of this publication may be reproduced in whole or in part without written permission of the publisher. For information regarding permission, write to Bellwether Media, Inc., Attention: Permissions Department, 6012 Blue Circle Drive, Minnetonka, MN 55343.

Library of Congress Cataloging-in-Publication Data

Names: Sabelko, Rebecca, author.
Title: Juneteenth / by Rebecca Sabelko.
Description: Minneapolis, MN : Bellwether Media, Inc., 2023. | Series: Blastoff! Beginners: Happy holidays! | Includes bibliographical references and index. | Audience: Ages 4-7 years | Audience: Grades K-1
Identifiers: LCCN 2022036391 (print) | LCCN 2022036392 (ebook) | ISBN 9798886871029 (Library Binding) | ISBN 9798886871906 (Paperback) | ISBN 9798886872286 (eBook)
Subjects: LCSH: Juneteenth--Juvenile literature.
Classification: LCC E185.93.T4 S24 2023 (print) | LCC E185.93.T4 (ebook) | DDC 394.263--dc23/eng/20220805
LC record available at https://lccn.loc.gov/2022036391
LC ebook record available at https://lccn.loc.gov/2022036392

Text copyright © 2023 by Bellwether Media, Inc. BLASTOFF! BEGINNERS and associated logos are trademarks and/or registered trademarks of Bellwether Media, Inc.

Editor: Christina Leaf   Designer: Laura Sowers

Printed in the United States of America, North Mankato, MN.

Table of Contents

It Is Juneteenth!	4
Freedom for All!	6
Family, Food, and Fun!	12
Juneteenth Facts	22
Glossary	23
To Learn More	24
Index	24

It Is Juneteenth!

Time for the **barbecue**.
Everyone enjoys red drinks.
It is Juneteenth!

barbecue

Freedom for All!

Juneteenth is on June 19. It is also called **Freedom** Day.

It honors Black people being freed from **slavery**. It began in Texas.

Juneteenth honors freedom. It honors Black history.

Family, Food, and Fun!

People go to church.
They sing.

church

People go to **parades**. They fly the Juneteenth flag.

parade

Juneteenth flag

Families and friends meet up. They eat red foods.

People learn about Black history.

Let's sing and dance! Happy Juneteenth!

Juneteenth Facts

Celebrating Juneteenth

friends
red foods
barbecue

Juneteenth Activities

go to church

fly the Juneteenth flag

eat red foods

Glossary

barbecue

an outdoor meal or party

freedom

able to live as one chooses

parades

people or groups who walk together during events

slavery

the act of people owning other people

To Learn More

ON THE WEB

FACTSURFER

Factsurfer.com gives you a safe, fun way to find more information.

1. Go to www.factsurfer.com.

2. Enter "Juneteenth" into the search box and click 🔍.

3. Select your book cover to see a list of related content.

Index

barbecue, 4, 5
church, 12, 13
dance, 20
drinks, 4
families, 16
flag, 14, 15
foods, 16
freedom, 8, 10
Freedom Day, 6
friends, 16
history, 10, 18
June, 6
parades, 14
sing, 12, 20
slavery, 8
Texas, 8

The images in this book are reproduced through the courtesy of: Hamara, cover; Xinhua/ Alamy, p. 3; Boston Globe/ Getty Images, pp. 4-5; ZUMA Press Inc/ Alamy, pp. 6-7, 14-15; Bob Daemmrich/ Alamy, pp. 8-9; Bastiaan Slabbers, pp. 10-11, 18-19; Brandon Bell/ Getty Images, pp. 12-13; Godofredo A. Vásquez/ AP Images, p. 14 (parade); TrotzOlga, p. 16; Jeffrey Isaac Greenberg 7+/ Alamy, pp. 16-17; Alexandra Wimley/ AP Images, pp. 20-21; Tetra Images/ Alamy, p. 22 (celebrating); FatCamera, p. 22 (go to church); EvgeniiAnd, p. 22 (fly the Juneteenth flag); Monkey Business Images, pp. 22 (eat red foods), 23 (barbecue, freedom); Tippman98x, p. 23 (parades); gameover/ Alamy, p. 23 (slavery).